Caught up in

The life of Kostas Matheou

1918 – 1943

By

Alexander Matheou

For my father, George Matheou

Table of Contents

Prologue

In my line of work I travel a great deal, and when I do, invariably I am asked where I am from. I reply that I am from England. Clearly, this is neither the expected nor a satisfactory response. My dark curly hair and Mediterranean features are scrutinised. Then comes the second question: but where are you really from? "England, but my father was born in Greece". This, it turns out, is a much better answer. The suspicious look turns into a smile: "ah, you're Greek!"

It is true, the Matheous were Greeks. Two generations ago, it would have been impossible for any Matheou descending from the elder Constantine, about whom this history begins, to imagine anything else. The Matheous lived in, died in and died for, Greece. Their life stories were deeply intertwined with events in the country around them.

Today, most of the Matheous from that line of the family are French or English, and the connection to our country of origin is receding ever further into the distance. My generation, the second, is still aware of its roots. We remember our grandmother, who although living in England, was still very much Greek. Our father still has early memories of Greece. As children, the gods and heroes of Greece would frequently come up at our dinner table and in bedtime stories.

Our own children though, feel that link far more tenuously. Their children may barely be aware of it at all. Soon, the memory and the connection could dissipate altogether.

Considering the colour, drama and tragedy of this family history – this would be a sad loss of heritage.

And it is all closer to us than we think. My father, alive and well in 2016, knew his grandfather, who helped capture Thessaloniki from the Ottoman Empire in 1913. He in turn knew his grandfather, who was born amongst musket fire and sword fights in villages devastated by plague during the Greek War of Independence in the 1820s. Distant times and places seem less distant when we realise just how closely connected we still are to the people who lived there.

Our grandparents and great grandparents looked like us. They probably shared many character traits, but the stories and values they cherished were different. This is a history of one member of the family, my grandfather, Kostas Matheou, whose short life was the stuff of family legend as we were growing up. But to understand his story we need to understand something about the lives of his parents, the wars they fought and the formative years of modern, Greek history that they lived through. These formed the stories and values that Kostas cherished, and in turn shaped how he lived, and died.

As crowded days fly by it is easy to make do with the snippets we hear about the tumultuous lives of our grandparents and not probe for more detail. But if we are not careful, when we do finally become curious, all the threads to lead us back there are gone. If I had tried to write this history even twenty years ago, there is so much more I could have learned. Now the protagonists have all passed away, and they have taken their stories with them.

This short history is a reconstruction based on what little we still know – from family memories passed down, from letters, postcards, photographs and newspaper articles. The story is extended by weaving these snippets of information into a narrative about events unfolding in Greece at the time. That way, the little we know can be brought back to life. To learn, for example, that three sons of the elder Constantine Matheou fought in the Asia Minor war of 1919–1922, is just an isolated, cold fact unless you explain why so many Greeks thought that disastrous war was worth fighting.

Originally, I had thought that I would just write this up, print it out, hand it around my family and leave it at that. Now I have taken it one step further and published it online. I suspect only a few people will read it, but then again, it is written for those few people: for the descendants of Constantine Matheou; those alive now and those not yet born. And given that those descendants are likely to become increasingly scattered around the world: this may be the one, last chance to capture this story, before it is forgotten forever.

One word of warning before we begin: a challenge of writing a family history about Greece is that the same names are passed down to every second generation – meaning that almost every character in this narrative is called either Constantine, George or Alexander. That can be confusing, so to make things easier, I refer to the founding member of the family, Constantine Matheou (born 1856) by his full name: Constantine, and his grandson, who is the main protagonist in this narrative, I refer to as Kostas –

the shortened version of his name used by his family and friends.

So now, to the story itself; which at its heart is an attempt to understand a fight or flight decision of a 25-year-old man, standing in the mountains of central Greece in October 1943, watching the Germans encircle his position. But to get to that moment, we have to start at the beginning.

I: The Pattern is Broken

In the spring of 1919, when Kostas was one years old, his father, George Matheou, kissed him goodbye and went to war. It was the third time he had been called to fight for Greece within seven years. This time though was different. This was the war that all Greeks had been dreaming of for a hundred years: the war that would restore to Greece its once mighty Christian capital – Constantinople.

George's father, the elder Constantine Matheou, bid his son farewell with a mixture of pride and deep trepidation. As a patriotic Greek, he could not help but be excited at the prospect of Greece finally realising its "megali idea" – the age long hope to reunite the Greeks of Byzantium into one, greater Greece. Yet his pride was tainted by a terrible fear of loss. Constantine had invested everything into his children. Within one generation he had broken the Matheous out of the trap of rural poverty and put them on a ladder to succeed as educated men and women, in cities, far from the dark, illiterate villages where he had spent his childhood.

Constantine, like almost all Greeks in the mid-1800s, had been born into poverty, into a new country that inherited some of Europe's most glorious history, but no schools, factories or roads.

His own father, another George Matheou, had been born in 1825, in the middle of the Greek War of Independence, amidst pillaging, burning, attacks from the Greeks, reprisals from the Turks and the devastation of plague. The family's home village, a hundred miles north of Athens in Lamia, around the market town of Atalanti, changed hands three times in the war that consumed Greece in the first years of his father's life. The numbers killed in these local battles were not huge, but even the death of 50 men is a great loss to a small community. In Atalanti there were only around 300 houses. A third of them were in the Turkish quarter. The violence was deeply personal. Everyone knew the Turkish families murdered in their homes. Everyone knew the Greeks slaughtered in reprisal once the Ottomans retook the town.

The War of Independence eventually liberated Greece from centuries of occupation, but with freedom came the daunting responsibility of state building in a country traumatised by violence and civil war, plagued by banditry, sparsely populated by small, remote communities speaking diverse dialects of Greek.

Yet slowly, as the decades passed, a country began to emerge. In Atalanti, the first primary school was founded in 1831. The first Greek boarding school opened in 1843. Five years after Constantine was born in 1856, the first road between Atalanti and the nearest town was constructed. By the time he was 29 years old, he saw the first oil lamps installed for lighting the town.

Constantine was determined to be part of this progress. In the years after the Ottomans were killed and expelled by the war, their land was handed out and divided among peasants so that no landed aristocracy could emerge. This was the foundation of the new democracy. It gave families such as the Matheous a platform on which to build more independent lives.

Still, for the most part, the rhythm and habits of village life rolled on unchanging, as they had for centuries past. Agricultural productivity was pitifully low, and most of the new landowners got by doggedly on subsistence agriculture; always aware that one failed harvest could lead to tragedy. Neighbourly support, endless toil and prayer were the three strategies designed to ward off the ever-present danger of starvation.

Constantine had higher aspirations for himself, but most of all for his children. He learned everything he could about the benefits of modern agricultural machinery, and introduced their use within the deeply conservative countryside. Once he made enough money, he bought more equipment, and then more, until he could make his living by renting out equipment that began to modernise and increase productivity for the people of Atalanti.

At the turn of the century, he built a large, two-storey house in the centre of town, at the foot of the hills towering over Atalanti, and crucially, close to the local school.

As his wealth grew, he was driven by one, all-consuming goal: that his children would not toil the land as he and his father had done. They would not know hunger. His children would be educated. They would live in cities. They would help shape the still young nation of Greece.

Together with his wife, Maria Tsolaki, Constantine had six boys and two girls. Now, in 1919, he was once again seeing his eldest son, George Matheou, off to war. George had been the first to break the mould of dependency on the land. He had graduated in classics from the

University of Athens; opening the door to a more comfortable life as a teacher.

Yet in Greece, in the early years of 20th Century, young men were expected to combine their jobs with military service, and if needed, to fight for their country. Already Constantine had seen three sons off to war in the last seven years. Thankfully, all had returned. He could only pray that this time too, George would do the same.

II: Forging a Family and a Nation

George Matheou, like all men of his generation, was a product of the Greek state building project that rested on three pillars – mass schooling, mass conscription and state control of the Orthodox Church.

Before the war of independence, identity in Greece had been more religious than national. You were Orthodox or you were Muslim. The mass schooling was designed to change this, and to give a new, common, national identity to the scattered communities across the fragmented country. It was dominated by Greek classics, Greek language and Greek history.

It was a history that needed to be rediscovered. The world of classical Athens was an inspiration to educated Europeans in the 1800s but had been long forgotten in illiterate, Ottoman occupied Greece. The ancient buildings were ignored, pillaged for stones or used for storage, and held in contempt by both Greek Orthodox and Muslims alike for the pagan history they represented.

That pagan history would now inspire Greek pride and shape Greeks' understanding of who they were and their place in the world. George's education, from primary right up to the University of Athens, was soaked in the ancient past: Homer's celebration of the glory and horror of war; Herodotus's telling of the defiance of the Spartans against the mighty Persian army at Thermopylae; Thucydides' sober descriptions of the brutality and tragedy of civil war; the philosophical enquiry of Plato and Aristotle.

George became joined to this journey of historical rediscovery when he married Alexandra Kaloudis, daughter of one of Greece's most renowned archaeologists, Panayiotis Kaloudis. Panayiotis was one of the many Greeks at the time committed to restoring the heritage of the ancient world. He worked on excavations of the Acropolis and the ancient stadium at Olympia. His proudest achievement was the reconstruction of the Lion of Chaeronea from its shattered and scattered remnants. The monument had been built to honour the sacrifice of the Sacred Band of Thebes at the Battle of Chaeronea, fought in 338 BC less than 50 miles from Atalanti. It was a pivotal clash that pitched Phillip II of Macedon and his son Alexander (the Great) against an alliance of southern states, led by Athens and Thebes. The victory of the Macedon army allowed Alexander to focus his attention on the conquest of Persia. The Lion of Chaeronea marked one of the most decisive battles of the ancient world.

George's family life would have been coloured by stories such as these.

In western Europe, Greek history appears to fizzle out as the Romans begin to dominate the Mediterranean, but George and his generation were taught a different narrative, in which the empire of Alexander the Great flowed seamlessly into the empire of Byzantium, and from its capital of Constantinople: Greek culture, Greek language and Greek Orthodoxy remained preeminent in the civilised world for another 1000 years.

Their version of history would have looked like this: the small communities of freedom-loving Greeks defied the might of the Persian Empire, and through their victories at Marathon and Salamis ushered in a golden age that gave the world democratic traditions, philosophy, science and some of its greatest art. Alexander took this culture east to the ends of the known world and made Greek the lingua franca of the largest empire ever known. When Rome fell to barbarian invasions it moved its capital east, to Greek-speaking Byzantium, where the Byzantine empire protected Europe from Tatar hordes, Persians and the new armies of Islam; until it was betrayed and ransacked by Catholic Christian crusaders; and became the obsession of the great Turkish conqueror, Sultan Mehmed II. As Mehmed II surrounded and bombarded Constantinople with giant cannons, the last Emperor, Constantine, reminded his soldiers that they were the descendants of the ancient Greek heroes, and he fought alongside them, valiantly, to his death, until the city finally fell in 1453. One by one the Greek islands followed, and finally the Greek mainland itself fell to the Turkish armies. Yet the Greeks never surrendered. For four centuries, the men took to the mountains and continued to fight until finally, in 1828, they succeeded in liberating part of their ancient homeland; but only part. The rest, the greater Greece, was still to be liberated: Crete, Thessaly, the Ionian islands, Cyprus, Salonika, and most of all – the Greeks of Asia Minor, the great Greek city of Smyrna and the capital of Christian Greece – Constantinople.

The restoration of greater Greece was the megali idea. It was an idea that mobilised and unified Greeks. It pervaded schooling, higher education, the army, the media, the church and politics. For George, it would have been an idea present throughout his life.

As a child in 1897, when George was just 12 years old, the megali idea had a serious setback when a thirty-day war with the Ottoman Empire resulted in Greece actually losing territory. But 15 years later, a new round of Balkans wars in 1912 and 1913 catapulted Greece into regional ascendency. This time, George was part of it.

It was the first time he was faced with the reality of battle. "I am missing you my darling Alexandra" he wrote to his wife on a postcard from Macedonia, "we are drunk on gunpowder and battle here, but even in the thick of fighting I miss you. Your name is always on my lips. I lie down on my stomach, shooting at the enemy, and even then I miss you."

From a military perspective, this war was perhaps the finest hour in Greece's modern history. Greece achieved a string of victories against the Ottoman forces. Most significantly, George and the Greek army secured the annexation of the ancient, multi-cultural city of Salonika. Crete soon followed. The Ottoman

Empire was crumbling, and the megali idea looked tantalisingly possible.

George returned back to Atalanti a hero, but within months the atmosphere in the Matheou household was again full of anticipation. World War 1 broke out in 1914. Constantine's eldest three sons, George, Pantelis and Anargiros, were all now mobilised for military service and waiting for news about whether, where and on what side, they would be deployed.

There were so many unknowns because Greece was crippled by a conflict between King Constantine, who was sympathetic to Germany, and its great republican leader, Venizelos, who was strongly inclined to side with Great Britain and France. The stalemate lingered throughout the first three years of the war, keeping Greece inactive and alienating it from its traditional allies. In the end, in 1917, Britain and France applied enough pressure to force the King to resign, and Venizelos began mobilising an army of 250 000 men. Both George and his younger brother Anargiros were called up: George as Lieutenant in the Infantry, Anargiros as a Lieutenant in the Calvary. They took to the field briefly, but effectively, in 1918.

After a humiliating, slow start to the war, Greece had in the last minute emerged triumphantly. Crucially, it had landed troops in the heart of the defeated and collapsing Ottoman Empire, and together with Allied forces, even temporarily entered Constantinople itself.

Venizelos shone during the peace negotiations in Versailles. He worked to extract as many territorial gains for Greece as possible, and he succeeded. Most importantly, he secured international approval to occupy the Greek dominated port city of Smyrna, in Asia Minor, in May 1919. The question of who would eventually take control of Constantinople itself remained open, but it all seemed to be going Greece's way. Or so it seemed.

The mood in Greece was buoyant with patriotism. Every schoolchild in Greece had been taught of the cruel occupation of the Turks and how the occupation continued to this day in Asia Minor. The newspapers rallied the national indignation and the call for justice.

After University, George had become a teacher of classics and then headmaster of the school in Atalanti. He probably told children the same stories about the suppression of the Greeks by the Turks and the unfinished mission to liberate Greeks everywhere. Yet he was also a solider, and very much part of Greece's second pillar of nation building – mass conscription. He had been mobilised on and off for ten years. In May 1919, he was therefore expecting the call up to go to Asia Minor.

This time though, he received exemption papers instead. As the eldest son in a large family, the Greek government expected George to stay at home and manage the household, and instead the conscription papers were sent to the second oldest son in the family – Pantelis Matheou.

George, however, knew just how little his younger brother, Pantelis, was cut out for war. So he gave his exemption papers to Pantelis, and prepared to go to Asia Minor in his place.

Captain George Matheou was 31 years old in 1919. His demeanour was already formal, with a touch of coldness. He was father to one child, his son, Kostas, but his wife, Alexandra, was already pregnant with their second child. If there was any relish at the chance of being part of realising Greece's megali idea, it must have been tempered by a painful awareness of how much he now had to lose.

Alexandra, unlike many Greek women seeing their husbands off to this long awaited war, at least had the small comfort of coming from wealth. Yet even with money the prospect of widowhood in Greece was a bleak one. Beyond the personal loss, young widows were condemned to a life of mourning, shrouded in black.

Alexandra may have been proud that George was protecting his younger brother. She may have been angry that he had volunteered to leave her. She almost certainly filled the house with icons of saints carefully selected to intercede to protect her husband. When George finally left his home, his uniform would have been permeated with incense that burned to carry prayers for his safety.

III: The Asia Minor War

At first, it was just as George and the Greek army imagined it would be. It was May 15th, 1919, and under the cover of darkness, at around 2am, 18 Greek warships, carrying 18 000 infantrymen, 4000 animals and 750 cannon landed in Smyrna. As dawn broke the disembarking soldiers were greeted by crowds of ecstatic Greeks, who had come out in the night waving torches and Greek flags, singing the Greek anthem to welcome their liberators.

For the Greek army, this was a long awaited reunion. There were more Greeks living in Smyrna than in Athens. Greek merchants and businessmen dominated the culture and economy of the city. Of 4600 factories and shops in Smyrna, 4000 were owned by the Anatolian Greeks. This, they believed, was liberation, not conquest.

Yet at the same time as the Greek army marched proudly through the cheering crowds in the port, in the Turkish quarter, the town criers woke the faithful with the terrible news: their homeland was now under occupation.

The town looked and felt Greek, but it wasn't. At the turn of the century, Smyrna's population was about 50% Greek, but by 1919, refugees from the Balkan wars and the First World War had increased Turkish migration into the city, and most people living there that May would not have seen the Greeks as liberators.

Still, within those first months in 1919, the Ottoman army was in disarray, and there was no serious opposition to the vastly superior Greek forces. The Greeks secured Smyrna, and skirmished successfully to secure the surrounding towns as a border. Then George and the army waited for orders about what to do next.

With the Greeks now in charge, news and rumours of the appalling treatment of Ottoman Christians by the Turks over the last six years could circulate widely. George and the Greek army heard stories about massacres, deportations, executions, rapes, burning of entire villages, the destruction of Greek monasteries and churches, the formation of labour brigades from amongst Greek men, who were then beaten and starved to death by Turkish officers. They heard of Greek women being driven into harems, of torture, and the sale of young girls for a few cents each. In terms of numbers, the worst stories came from the Christian Armenians, who had been massacred in their hundreds of thousands between 1913 and 1916. The exact figures have been disputed ever since, but at the time newspapers were claiming that 1.5 million Armenians had been murdered and over half a million Greeks. The Greek army, gangs of Greek and Armenian civilians, were fuming and restless for revenge.

The Greek hold on Smyrna was militarily secure for the time being, but while the legality of Greece's claim was still being hammered out in the corridors of power in Europe, a new force of Turkish nationalism was emerging under the defiant leadership of Mustafa Kemal. By 1920, it was becoming clear that Kemal, soon to be known as Attaturk, was going to be a force to be reckoned with. He had no intention of giving up Turkish land without a fight.

Feeling that the tide of events might be turning against them, British Prime Minister Lloyd George and Venizelos decided that British and Greek interests needed to be advanced now while Greece still had the military upper hand, and so in June 1920, the Greek army was ordered to deepen its invasion into Anatolia.

Captain George Matheou was part of a force of 120 000 that began to trek across the Anatolian desert to confront and destroy Kemal's resistance. Kemal's national base was the city of Ankara, 320 miles from Smyrna. To get there, dozens of towns and villages would have to be secured en-route, by force. As a classicist, George must have begun this journey with the invigorating sense that he was part of an ancient line of armies crossing these steppes from the Greek mainland. Just over three thousand years before, the legendary alliance of Greek states had landed in Anatolia to sack Troy. Just over two thousand years before, Alexander the Great had led his armies through Anatolia, passing close to where Ankara was located, where he had famously cut the Gordian knot. That invasion had laid the foundations of the Hellenization of Asia Minor, which in turn justified the great reclaiming of the lands taking place now.

Yet the further George and the Greek army moved from Smyrna itself, the harder it was to imagine Anatolia as part of Greece. They may have been issued identity cards with maps that claimed Anatolia as part of the new, greater homeland, but as they marched through the villages and towns, dominated by Minarets and dusty Eastern markets, what they saw was a Turkish culture, hosting a Greek minority.

Perhaps they had imagined an Asian, Turkish domination over an enslaved, European, Christian people. Instead, what George and the Greek army encountered were largely one people, some of whom had over the years adopted Islam, while some had stayed Christian. The two cultures had diverged, but co-existed, for the most part peacefully.

This makes what happens next all the harder to understand. As the Greek army occupied villages and towns deeper into Anatolia, they burned and destroyed them, and committed atrocities against the people that lived there. Diplomats, reporters and missionaries living in Anatolia saw the deadly effects of Greek violence. Soon their stories were being published across Europe. The tide of European public opinion in support of Greece slowly began to turn.

In many cases it was not actually the Greek army, at this stage anyway, that was committing the worst of these atrocities. There were plenty of irregular armed groups of Armenians and Greeks thirsting for vengeance, hanging around on the periphery, quick to seize the opportunity of the Greek offensive to pillage and burn. But all too often the Greek army either participated or turned a blind eye, and the idea that this was an army of liberation was fast losing credibility. We cannot know now what George thought of all of this, or how he was involved or behaved, but by autumn 1920, he had been in the thick of combat, and exposed to acts of terrible barbarity.

The Greek advance was steady, but the politics back in Greece were not. The war was losing support at home and abroad. Venizelos was crushed in elections in November 1920. His ally, King Alexander, had died from a monkey bite that turned septic in October, and King Constantine, whose abdication had been forced in 1916, was returned to the throne. King Constantine hated Venizelos but he had no intention of ending the war, whatever the public mood. He believed the Greeks fighting in Asia

Minor were on sacred mission to preserve and rekindle the land's ancient, Hellenic civilisation.

The war now though would have to be pursued without the certainty of British support. Lloyd George was increasingly exposed and alone in believing the Greek cause should be backed and resourced. His inability to mobilise assistance both isolated and weakened the Greek army, who could not hope to sustain essential supply chains so deep into Anatolia. To make matters worse, King Constantine wanted to bring in a new generation of officers, whose primary loyalty would be to him, not to the republican sympathies of Venizelos.

It was probably around this time, as a result of this new call up, that Constantine Matheou's third son, Anargiros, and his fourth son, Alexander, arrived in Asia Minor. George's heart must have sunk to think of Alexander, who had just turned 20 years old, being exposed to the brutality of this campaign. Anargiros was at least a Captain with experience from the First World

War. Alexander was just beginning his life, following his father's dream that he would pursue higher education, studying law in Athens, and looking forward to becoming the first lawyer in the family. Just before he left to Asia Minor, Alexander put in his papers to apply for the third year of his course.

It appears also that around this time, and perhaps because two of his brothers had been conscripted, that George was discharged, and returned back to Atalanti. He had been in Asia Minor for nearly two years and his fighting days were now over. He had survived again. The full brutality of this war though was about to fall onto the shoulders of Anargiros and Alexander.

IV: The Great Catastrophe

So it happened, that without allies, and with hundreds of inexperienced new officers, the campaign into Anatolia continued its push towards Ankara. King Constantine arrived in Smyrna that summer and declared that it was time to cut the Gordian knot – to reach, as Alexander the Great had done, the deep heart of Anatolia, and strike a decisive blow.

There were a series of strategic towns, each surrounded by dozens more villages, to secure before an attack could be made on Ankara. With each one the resistance stiffened. The months passed. Supply lines thinned. The land became ever more arid and rocky. The trucks, carts, horses and lines of marching men kicked up thick clouds of dust. The sun was relentless. Water was scarce. The ground too hard to build deep trenches and when the firing started, men lay in shallow ditches to keep cover and return fire. When it was time to advance, Captain Anargiros Matheou and Lieutenant Alexander Matheou would have led their men, running across flat plains, cannon shattering the air, shells exploding around them, bullets whizzing past their ears, the panicked cries of fallen men mixed into the chaotic roar of battle. The enemy was attacked with cannon, then guns, and finally bayonets. One by one the towns fell, until, in August 1921, the Turkish army retreated behind the banks of the River Sakarya.

The Matheou brothers and the Greek army were now just 40 miles from Ankara. Anargiros scribbled a quick postcard to George. "Here's a note to remind you of your campaigning days. I am near Ankara. Say hello to all the family in Atalanti." In Athens, the Greek government spoke of imminent victory. The fighting was exhausting and brutal, but the Greeks were still better armed and had a slight numerical superiority over the Turkish army, and until this point, the Greeks had won every engagement they had fought.

The tide, however, was turning. Kemal decided that he would make his last stand on the banks of Sakarya. He ordered a massive mobilisation of the population. Those who could fight would have to fight. Those who couldn't fight were asked to share food, animals, equipment, clothes. This was a population whose homeland and culture were under attack, and the people mobilised to Kemal's call. His army swelled with fresh recruits. Women, children and the elderly carried supplies to the soldiers and blessed their courage. Equipment and weapons arrived for Kemal's army from the new Union of Soviet Republics, and from England's European rivals – France and Italy.

The Greek army however was alone, exhausted, its supply chains stretched. Throughout the last month they had fought for ground mile by mile, one bloody day at a time. The terrain was mountainous. The trucks, horses, cannons and carts had to be dragged up and down treacherous, rocky slopes. To surround the

Turkish positions around Sakarya, the Greeks extended their front lines across longer and longer distances, and by mid-August, the thinning front lines were stretched over 75 miles.

The Turkish army dug in on the high ground of the hills surrounding the banks of Sakarya, and to advance, the Greek army would have to storm and take these heights. For ten days and nights they fought, with cannons, guns, bayonets. The Greeks would storm the hills, capture them, be pushed back, and then capture them again. A Greek lithograph of the time portrays something of the horror – the exploding shells, the howling of the wounded, soldiers trampling over the lifeless bodies of their friends to hack at the enemy with cold steel, frenzied dogs feeding on the dead.

Finally, the Greeks stormed and captured the highest peak in the area, and Anargiros and Alexander may have caught a glimpse of the lights of Ankara, flickering dimly in the distance.

But as the Greek army won the heights, the Turkish cavalry began to focus on the rear supply lines of the overstretched Greek forces. They attacked and destroyed supply columns, and the Greeks, bloodied, exhausted and victorious on the highlands, were left without food, medicine for the wounded, or weapons to continue the attack. For the rest of his life George would lament that the war was lost by the failure to secure supplies, not failure on the battlefield.

On September 10th, Kemal launched a ferocious counter attack, and by September 11th, the Greeks had withdrawn to the south of the river, leaving thousands of dead on the battlefield.

The demoralised Greek army organised itself into a defensive line and a stalemate ensued. Greece had lost the capacity to advance but it still believed it could hold the territory it had occupied. The Greek government was desperate to secure military aid from the British, but received none. The Turkish army however, continued to boost its capacity with Soviet assistance.

The months passed, the Greeks looked ever more isolated, and sensing momentum was now his side, in August 1922, Kemal ordered his "Great Offensive" to destroy the Greek army.

On 25th August, the Turkish army crashed into the Greek defences and was repelled only after a day of bloody fighting. The Greeks line had held, but only just, and the fight was slipping out of them. They were far from home. They had ventured too deep into a land where they were unwelcome and hated. They had become what they despised. Their allies had abandoned them. They had little left to fight for. They now faced an enemy with everything to fight for.

The next day, the battle resumed, but it was all over for the Greeks. The defensive line was overrun. The army decisively defeated. Half of its soldiers captured or killed. Its equipment abandoned on the battlefield.

There was only one thing to do now: to get out of Anatolia, as quickly as possible.

At first the retreat was orderly, but discipline was breaking down, and each solider was consumed by just one thought – to get home alive. They retreated the way they had come, through towns and villages that they had sacked once, and that now they burned to the ground as part of a scorched earth strategy to deny everything to the pursuing Turkish army. They would leave only desert behind them.

They destroyed railways, bridges and roads. They plundered and stole everything they could as they retreated, filling their bags with old clothes, pots, pans and pieces of pottery they hoped were Hellenic antiques. Then they put the towns to flames.

For the people who lived in these towns, the Greek retreat was the most horrific part of the war. Towns that once housed tens of thousands of people were reduced to burnt out shells, reeking of the scorched flesh of those trapped inside the burning buildings. Photographs of the few survivors portray something of the horror. Flattened buildings, blackened corpses, shocked faces, parents weeping for murdered sons and abducted daughters. Again, we do not know if Anargiros or Alexander tried to stop this or if they were part of it – but for sure they saw it, in all its horror.

For the Anatolian Greeks living in these towns, it was not safe to stay to face the advancing Turkish army, not after the Greek army had wreaked such destruction. So they grabbed what little they could carry, and a giant exodus of an ancient people began. The Greek army retreated, and behind them, tens of thousands of women, children, elderly, men, carts, donkeys – all heading for the one place they thought they would be safe, the Greek city of Smyrna.

As Smyrna filled with refugees, Anargiros and the Greek army veered north for evacuation to mainland Greece, and he received terrible news. His young brother, Alexander, had been captured.

There was no more information. He was never seen again. There was no way to know if Alexander had died quickly, or in the primitive hospitals where the most severely wounded patients were now being left behind, or even worse in long captivity, in the sweltering, cramped prisons that were mushrooming behind the advancing Turkish army, or in the labour battalions, where Greek men were beaten and worked to death. There was only one thing for sure: Alexander had died far from his loved ones, in a failed war, probably terrified, and when his life should have been just beginning.

The Turkish cavalry entered Smyrna on a Saturday morning, September 9th. The next day Mustafa Kemal himself arrived and declared that non-combatants would not be harmed. His troops though, had other ideas. The Greeks and Armenians gathered in their tens of thousands on the port looking for ships on which they could escape. A fire broke out in the Armenian quarter, and soon the whole city was ablaze, with flames two miles long and a hundred feet high. Ships moored nearby watched in horror as the sky turned into a red glow. For four days and nights the city burned. The frantic screaming of the Greeks and Armenians could be heard for miles. They were clubbed and hacked to death in the chaos. They leapt into the sea and drowned. They were tormented by the fleeing rats scurrying in panic around their feet.

During the four days, over 50 000 Greeks and Armenians were burned to death, drowned or murdered in the fire. When the flames died down, the city of Smyrna was gone. Greek women, children and elderly were ordered to leave Anatolia forever. The men were conscripted into labour battalions and sent back to rebuild the towns the Greek army had destroyed. Less than 10% of these men survived. The megali idea was dead. Anatolia would never be Greek again.

V: A Family in Shock

Anargiros returned home to a family and to a country in shock. His arrival was followed by 1.5 million Greek refugees from Asia Minor, who suddenly made up 20% of Greece's population. They settled in the countryside across northern Greece, but also crowded around Athens and Piraeus, forming impoverished, urban slums. They brought with them the trauma of displacement, but also new cuisines, music, entrepreneurship and a more advanced knowledge of industry and agriculture. Greece's megali idea would now be about inclusion rather than expansion.

His parents, Constantine and Maria, could meet him with a mix of relief and tears, deeply happy that one son had survived, but traumatised by the uncertainty surrounding Alexander's death. His brother George though, was probably the only one who could truly understand what Anargiros had lived through.

George now had two children – his son Kostas and a daughter Heraklia, and Alexandra was expecting their third child. In 1923 she gave birth to a second daughter, Maria, named after George's mother. Perhaps the brutality that George had witnessed at the hands of men darkened his views of male nature, because he seemed far less able to express affection to his sons than his daughters. With Kostas, and later in life with his second son, Alexander, George maintained a distance, but he doted on his daughters.

Maria's life though, was tragically short. In her second year she fell ill, and no amount of prayer or medical advice seemed to help. In 1925 she died, still not two years old. George and Alexandra were heartbroken. It was perhaps the loss of Maria that tormented Alexandra with a lifelong fear that her remaining children would be taken away by sickness. At the first sign of any ailment, she would rush to bring out icons and to fill the room with incense, reciting prayers to bring holy protection to her child.

George reacted in a different way. He was not one to be emotional, but whenever Kostas, Heraklia, and later Alexander (born 1925) and Nafsika (born 1928) were sick, he would sit all night if need be, sometimes besides their beds, sometimes quietly behind the bedroom door, until the child recovered. He cared, but he was not good at showing it.

His reserve gave the Matheou home an air of formality. This may have been a character trait or the product of his years in the military, but it may also have been a reaction to all that he had seen and lived through in the three wars that he had fought. It could have not have been easy to carry within him the traumas of the Asia Minor war, to recall and relive the bloodshed and barbarity and then look around him and to see Greece shun the incident as "the Great Catastrophe". He had fought, as it turns out, not for his son Kostas to inherit the megali idea, but the shame of defeat. His brother, Alexander, hadn't died to build a future for Greeks everywhere, but to confine Greeks forever to the arid, small tip of their once great empire, that now became the permanent borders of Greece. How was he supposed to weave that into the glorious, hopeful history that he had taught at school before the war? How was he supposed to explain what happened to the children?

Who was to blame became a dominant theme in Greek politics in the 1920s. Even though the republican Venizelos had started the war, the popular reaction was to blame the King, who had taken over command mid-way and was therefore seen as responsible for losing it. In 1924, the King was asked to abdicate for the second time, and the Second Hellenic Republic was proclaimed. Not though, with unanimous support. The foundations of the divides that would fracture Greek politics in the coming decades were forming now: an increasingly political army;

tensions between those who believed Greece should be a monarchy and those who believed in the republic; fermenting communist sympathies, particularly among the disgruntled, Anatolian Greeks.

George's school in Atalanti was not large. A school photograph from the early 1920s shows the children as formal and as presentable as they can make themselves, in a motley mix of their best dresses and blazers. George is sitting in the centre, holding a wriggling Kostas, staring intensely. The "Great Catastrophe" aside, the lessons in Greek history, literature and language continued. Greece would now have a different destiny than the one George had anticipated before leaving to Anatolia, but it could still be a great one, and that greatness would still build on the foundations that made Greece's past so glorious: a love of freedom and a fierce determination to protect that freedom. These were lessons that would make deep impressions on young Kostas.

In 1926, George's mother, Maria, died. George had lost his brother, his daughter and now his Mother, in the space of just four years. As he talked the school children through the texts of Homer, he perhaps found comfort in Odysseus's words: "Bear patiently my heart, for you have suffered heavier things".

VI: Life and Tragedy in Athens

By 1930, the elder, now widower, Constantine Matheou had every reason to feel proud. He had risen from humble beginnings, accumulated wealth, contributed to the welfare of his town and its surrounding villages. His house stood tall and proud in the centre of Atalanti. Most important of all though – his sons had fulfilled the high aspirations he had held for them. George was a teacher and a war hero. Anargiros was a cavalry officer and war hero. Emmanuel (Manolis) had graduated top of his class at the Naval College was now a Lieutenant Commander. The youngest, Evangelos, was also an officer, and was just about to enter the newly formed Aviation force. Constantine had envisaged a life for his children different from the one he had known as a child – a more independent, urban, sophisticated life, and he had achieved his dream. He had lost one son, and more tragedy was around the corner, but for now, he could feel content. Apart from one, niggling fact – there was one son that just wouldn't comply with his father's wishes – his second son, Pantelis Matheou.

Pantelis also served in a war like his brothers. He was conscripted in 1913 and officially served until 1919. His service though was quite unique. The details are a little vague, but it appears that around 1916, before Greece had committed troops to fight in World War 1, Pantelis's regiment encountered a Hungarian force on the Greek border, allied to the Germans. The leader of Pantelis's group was loyal to the King and thereby sympathetic to the Germans, and opposed to Venizelos, who was determined to bring Greece into war on the side of UK and France. Perhaps because of this, they surrendered to the Hungarians and were duly transported to eastern Germany (now western Poland).

As they had surrendered willingly and showed no antipathy towards the Germans, their captivity was a mild one. Pantelis and his fellow soldiers, who were mostly peasant farmers anyway, were allotted land and told to farm. Some restriction of movement was placed upon them, but apart from that, they lived comfortable lives, produced a local newspaper in Greek, and mingled freely with the local population.

When the war ended with German defeat, Pantelis made his way back home. As his war experience paled in comparison to those of his battle weary brothers, George and Anargiros, it was generally kept quiet. But when on the subject, Pantelis would recall nostalgically just what a nice time he had in eastern Germany, and just how many little Matheous must be running around those German villages by now.

Pantelis was a kind-hearted man, but as he settled back into life in Atalanti, he showed no inclination to study like his brothers. His father, Constantine, despaired and harassed him constantly, asking him again and again "but what will you do when I die?" Pantelis would give a repartee reply, that "when that day comes, I'll work it out." His father, however, could not leave it at that. He gathered his children together in Atalanti and explained the situation. All his children were now educated and independent. Their future would not depend on the land, and it would not be based in Atalanti. The one exception was Pantelis, so why not let him inherit the family business and the family home, and let the rest of the children pursue their careers in Athens? This, in turn, is what happened, and was happening naturally anyway. Pantelis and his descendants were the only branch of the family to stay in the ancestral base of Atalanti. His grandson, another Pantelis Matheou, still lives in the same home until this day. For the rest of the Matheous, as Constantine had predicted, their futures lay in Athens and beyond.

Athens was a better place to get the education that George and Alexandra wanted to give to their own children: their daughters and their sons. George got a job in a new school, and the family moved into a comfortable apartment near the centre of Athens.

The Athens of the 1930s, in the centre at least, would look very familiar to modern Athenians. Beneath the Acropolis, the Plaka was full of restaurants and cafes where the Athenians loved to pass their days and evenings. Monastiraki was abuzz with shops and stalls. Syntagma Square already had the same classic buildings as it does today. There were only a few cars, but the roads and boulevards were busy with an endless stream of trams. The ancient temples and monuments, once neglected and despised, were now a source of pride. The Parthenon was still a burned out shell in the 19th century, but by 1930, it was cleaned up, and it towered above the Athenians, as it had done for nearly 2500 years.

Those living close to the centre, like George and his family, often lived in apartments. Such apartments dated from the 1930s are now the most sought after in 21st Century Athens. But in the 1930s, you only had to turn a corner to see a different world. The backstreets were narrow and unpaved. People carried their wares on horses and carts. Families lived together in one room and collected water from nearby, communal taps. The worst conditions were in Piraeus, which still had the look and feel of giant refugee camp for Anatolian Greeks. Open sewers flowed through the streets. Families were crammed together in tiny rooms. At night, it was pitch dark and dangerous.

For young Kostas, going to school in Athens was probably more exciting than going to school in Atalanti, but that didn't mean that he enjoyed it. He was impatient with studies and struggled to value lessons that didn't have practical application. He excelled though at athletics and loved to hear stories about the deeds of Greek heroes. These deeds were still the stuff that Greek education was made of. The heroes of the classical world and the heroes of the War of Independence both protected Greece and defined its character.

Athenians were encouraged to see history not as a dry, distant subject, but as a bridge, leading to the Greece of today. Open-air classes were held in the same places that Socrates taught. The plays of Sophocles were performed for modern Athenians in the same theatres that they were premiered in over two thousand years before.

The ancient world had always been part of daily life for Kostas's mother, Alexandra, who had been brought up surrounded by stories and artefacts from the distant past. Together with her classicist husband, she probably imbued her children with a fascination with their Greek inheritance. Above all things, Alexandra doted on her eldest son; but for George, Kostas's lack of enthusiasm for schooling may have been a source of tension and anguish.

George, the headmaster and classicist, was the serious, older child, and his brother, Evangelos, the playful, younger one. Evangelos was 20 years younger than George, and only 10 years older than Kostas. He had none of George's formality and reserve. He was life loving, cheerful and particularly happy in female company. Yet, somehow, these youngest and eldest brothers, were still close.

Evangelos's eyes were on the future not the past. Aviation forces were not new in the 1930s, but they were still a novelty. There was great excitement when Prime Minister Venizelos announced the formation of a Greek Aviation Ministry in 1930, as a new, third branch of the armed forces. It possessed only a handful of fighter planes, but Venizelos knew that future battles would be won or lost in the skies, and he wanted Greece to be ready. For that he needed pilots – young, daring men who would be willing to take extraordinary risks to master the use of these fighter planes. Evangelos was such a young man. He graduated in 1930 and immediately applied to be a pilot. He obtained his licence in 1932 and within a year was a qualified instructor.

On 8th January 1934, he invited his older brother George to watch him practise his skills above an airfield outside Athens in a test to demonstrate the use of the plane's machine guns. George watched the aeroplane conduct the exercise. Then he watched the aeroplane enter into a spin and spiral towards the earth. It exploded on contact, killing Evangelos immediately. He was just 26 years old.

For a short while, in death, Evangelos became a national hero. His face was on the front page of Greek newspapers. His funeral was a national event. The Matheous stood at the front of the church, while the new Prime Minister, Panayis Tsaldaris, and his top government officials, came and expressed their condolences. Evangelos had given his life in an effort to make Greece stronger. The country loved and honoured him. Sixteen years old Kostas watched and learned, dreaming of sacrifice and glory.

The Matheous were in deep shock at the death of Evangelos, but the losses only continued. That same year, Constantine's third son, Anargiros, also died. He was 39 years old. By the end of 1934, three of Constantine's six sons were dead.

This left George as the only Matheou brother living in Athens. George's children remembered growing up in this household in different ways. The youngest son, Alexander, recalled creeping up the stairs towards the apartment with his boots in his hand so as not to make any noise that may disturb his strict and daunting father. His daughters recalled a more relaxed atmosphere.

George was kinder to his daughters than his sons, and generally more at ease with women than with men. This ease would lead him astray from time to time. In response, his wife, Alexandra, would feign terrible nightmares, and in the night she would find herself lashing out at George with her nails, teeth and legs. George would wake up: cut, bruised and alarmed, and would shake Alexandra gently, stroking her hair and telling her to wake up. Alexandra would mumble her apologies, turn over and fall asleep with a satisfied smile on her lips.

In 1934 George was 46 years old and rooted. Despite his firmness, there was one thing that he held deeply sacred: his children's right to choose what they wanted to do with their own lives. His responsibility was to see them educated. From then on, it was up to them. For his eldest son, Kostas, there appears to have been no doubt about what he would choose. As soon as he finished school, he entered the *Scholi Evelpidon*, the Hellenic Military Academy.

VII: Scholi Evelpidon

Kostas's school friend, K. Abrahams, later wrote that "Kostas joined the army as a way to distinguish himself." He was said to be always looking for ways to test his own character, to step into a storm to see how he would handle it. He was described as having fiery black eyes that left you frozen if they stared at you. His handshake felt like the grip of a vice. He was direct, honest and decisive. "When he said yes or no" wrote Abrahams, "you knew it was final." Yet behind what Abrahams describes as a manliness, that made him both a respected and beloved friend, there was sensitivity too. He wanted to be appreciated by others. He wanted to earn their respect. There was also warmth. He had a ready smile and took pleasure in supporting others.

He showed no inclination towards politics and considered it inferior to higher callings of honour and self-betterment. This probably made Kostas's army experience difficult, as in the 1930s, the Greek military had become extremely political.

Greece, like the rest of Europe, was hurt by the Great Crash of 1929. The economic pain gave rise to more right-wing politics and a growing demand for the restoration of the monarchy. The election of 1933 pushed Venizelos and his liberal party out of power, and a purge of his loyal military officers appeared imminent. In response, army officers loyal to Venizelos launched coups in 1933 and again in 1935. Both failed. In 1935, 60 officers were sentenced to death and over a 1000 were tried for conspiracy. This in turn left an army in place much more sympathetic to the return of the king.

That year, a group of high-ranking officers demanded that Prime Minister Tsaldaris, who had met the Matheou family the year before, either agree to the restoration of the monarchy or resign. He chose the latter. His replacement abolished the republic, and King George II, who had spent the last 12 years in exile in England, ascended to the throne for the second time.

At this time, Hitler had already been in power in Germany for two years and Mussolini in Italy for twelve. Stalin had his iron grip on the Soviet Union. War was not yet inevitable, but it was a time of radical nationalism, aggressive rhetoric, of intolerance of dissent, and of mobilising the masses to be fanatically loyal. Greece was not immune to these trends sweeping across Europe. In 1936, General Innonnis Metaxas, Greece's new leader, impatient with the trappings of parliamentary democracy, abandoned it and declared the "Regime of the Fourth of August 1936".

It was a dictatorship, but one that was milder in nature than those of Germany and Italy. Metaxas called it the Third Hellenic Civilisation. The first was ancient Greece, the second medieval Byzantium, and the third would be what he would build in modern Greece, which would combine the Pagan values of Sparta with the

Christian values of Byzantium. Like the regimes in Italy and Germany, he encouraged a culture of sacrifice for the nation, of loyalty, of discipline and of a hatred of communism. He policed this culture with active surveillance and arrested those who dared dissent.

In scale, his oppression was minor compared to the fascist and communist regimes of the time, but it was nevertheless repellent to many freedom loving Greeks, and deadly serious to those taken from their homes in the night to be beaten and tortured into submission. The dictatorship polarised Greece even further. There were, however, those who it was designed to benefit: most of all the loyal military, and the officer class, who were instilled with a pride of purpose, and reminded constantly of their duty to embody the heritage of classical Greece – to be the small nation that finds the honour and the courage to resist and defeat far larger adversaries.

This then, was the Greece of Kostas's formative years – a country of fascist salutes and enforced order, protected by an army drilled with lessons of Greek loyalty and sacrifice. There is no record of Kostas's opinions on this politics, if he had any. He was said to be fiercely independent and to find any form of slavery abhorrent. These values later clashed violently with life under occupation. But it is not evident that they were offended by Metaxas.

When joining the Academy in 1938, Kostas had to decide where exactly to enrol. He chose to follow the example of his uncle, Lieutenant Commander Manolis Matheou, who was studying electrical engineering in Paris. Kostas therefore enrolled into the engineering corps: a decision that was to make him later valuable to the Greek resistance.

Kostas joined the Academy together with his friend from Lamia, Nikolas Makarezos, who had now become fiancé to Kostas's sister, Heraklia Matheou. Years later, Nikolas Makarezos would form part a military junta that would take over Greece in response to a supposed communist threat, using forms of propaganda and repression similar to the Metaxas era. Ironically, this would in turn lead to the final abolishment of the monarchy in Greece and the founding of the Third Hellenic Republic.

But that was all 30 years in the future, and in 1938, Kostas and Nikolas, full of youthful optimism, could not envisage all that lay ahead. Like all Greeks though, they knew they were living in deeply uncertain times. War was brewing, and Greece was vulnerable. Kostas's training was accelerated. His three year course was condensed into two. Greece would need as many officers as it could muster.

Metaxas was trying to maintain cordial relations with all powers, but he knew that if push came to shove, Greece would stand by Great Britain. He refused to order a mobilisation so as not to unnerve the Axis Powers, but quietly, he ordered the prepositioning of weapons and the bolstering of defensive lines around Greece's land borders.

The Second World War broke out on 1st September 1939. France fell eight months later. Metaxas called up all reservists. Kostas by now would have been on high alert. On 15th August 1940, Italy torpedoed the Greek warship, Eli. Greece was outraged, but it was not yet a declaration of war.

On 20th October, Mussolini ordered his army to fabricate a security incident on the Albanian border during the coming week. A few Albanians were dressed up as Greeks and told to attack an Italian checkpoint in Italian occupied Albania. They did, and were duly shot to make it look authentic. Mussolini then ordered his forces to invade Greece with "maximum decisiveness and violence."

On 28th October, at 6am, Kostas was woken by the sound of air raid sirens ringing throughout Athens. It was now his generation's turn to fight.

VIII: "Heroes Fight like Greeks"

In the early hours of that morning, on 28th October 1940, Prime Minister Metaxas was woken by the Italian Ambassador. The Ambassador began awkwardly to list grievances against Greece and then demanded a series of impossible territorial concessions. Legend has it that the Prime Minister answered with one word: ohi. No. So it was war.

The day of 28th October was unforgettable for the Greeks who lived through it. The air sirens rang out at 6am. Crowds began to fill the streets. Newspapers rushed out special editions. Defiant broadcasts from Metaxas rang out from loud speakers. By mid-morning, the streets were teeming with people cheering, waving flags and chanting "ohi". Young men rushed from their homes and their workplaces to sign up to fight. Greece had not wanted to be drawn into this war, but now it was here, the prospect was met with defiance and patriotism.

Kostas, and his fellow officers and cadets, were surely part of these throbbing crowds, overflowing with a common conviction that Greece must be defended. His parents, George and Alexandra, were probably more circumspect: angry for Greece, fearful for what their son must now endure.

There is no record of what Kostas actually did on the Albanian front. Only that he was there, and according to his friend, that he "distinguished himself in sacrifice and courage." It is possible though to reconstruct broadly his experience based on the experiences of others.

There were around 100 000 Italian troops lined up along 250km frontier of rough, mountainous terrain. This invasion force faced initially around 50 000 Greeks, but mobilisation in Greece was increasing those numbers by the day, albeit with people with time only for only the briefest of training.

The terrain was brutal. The weather was filthy. The rivers were swollen with rain. Within days the men were layered in damp mud. The Greeks, perhaps with Kostas's help, blew up bridges to slow down the Italian advance.

The two armies clashed for the first time on 1st November, and the pattern of this battle was repeated over and again in the coming weeks. The Italians advanced to storm the high ground, in this case to seize the Gramala Hill, in an attempt to split the Greek defence in half. The next morning, the Greeks launched a counter attack. First, the Greek artillery opened fire. Then the Greeks fixed bayonets and charged up the hill. Junior officers, like Kostas, would run up first, clearing the way with hand grenades, before charging with bayonets and forcing the Italians back in violent hand-to-hand combat. Local peasants poured down from hills to cheer the Greeks on, taking a crack at any straggling Italians if they could. The Italians fell back, shocked by the determination and the viciousness of the Greek defence. It was only a small taste of what was to come.

With each day, the weather seemed to become ever more unbearable. The wind was penetrating. The soldiers were sinking in mud. Both sides had little to eat but bread and olives. The Italians were particularly poorly equipped. With the exception of one Alpine Regiment, they had not been trained for this sort of combat, or to live and fight in this cold, sleety landscape.

Very quickly, the momentum was on the side of the Greeks. They attacked with artillery, cavalry and then charged with bayonets to finish the job. Within two weeks the Italian's elite Alpine forces were all but crushed. On 14th November, after a three-hour battle, the Italian line was broken, and the Greek advance pushed the Italians back over the Albanian border.

A week after that, on 22nd November, the Greeks, and probably Kostas, entered the old Greek town of Korce in Albania. The ethnic Greek population rushed out to greet the Greek troops with open arms. In Athens, there was jubilation. Church bells rang. Crowds flocked into the streets. Strangers embraced. The Greeks had taken to this war in defiance, but as the underdog. They had committed to fight, but had hardly dared hope for victory. Yet now, not only were the Italians pushed back from Greek soil, but Greece was reliving the megali idea, and reclaiming lost territory into a greater Greece. For a brief moment, it seemed to the Greeks that they were living through a time as glorious as the victories of the classical era.

In Great Britain, Churchill was ecstatic. Someone else was finally standing up to the Axis powers, and they were actually winning. "From now on", he famously claimed, "it ought not to be said that Greeks fight like heroes, but that heroes fight like Greeks." That went down well in Athens.

For Kostas and those doing the fighting though, the most painful phase of this war was just beginning. The weather was worsening. The fog was thickening. The mountains were now capped with thick snow. Hunger and cold were becoming more deadly than the enemy. The temperatures dropped and by mid-December, frostbite became the worst killer in the war. A Battalion of 800 men could easily lose a third to this agonising form of death. Yet the fighting continued even in these conditions, and when the clashes ended, the dying postures of the soldiers were frozen in ice, and left like eerie carvings on the battlefield.

It was becoming ever harder to fight, not only because of this biting cold, but because the glorious, defensive phase of this war was won, and further advance lacked the mobilising sense of just cause. We do not know exactly where Kostas was at this time. It is only safe to say that somewhere on this Albanian front, like the other officers and soldiers of the Greek army, he was battle-hardened, tired, cold and hungry. He was just 22 years old.

IX: A Big Decision

There is a letter from Kostas written in January 1940, which indicates that he was in Athens at that time. It is not clear why. He may have been released to see his family. He may have been given a duty to organise civil defence. Bombings around Athens, and particularly in Piraeus, were happening daily. It is not clear if he stayed in Athens or went back to the Albanian front. Probably, it was the latter.

By this time, the Greek army had secured territory 30 miles in the east of Albania and 80 miles to the west. For now, the weather made further advances impossible.

The Greek army waited impatiently, entrenched, cold, restless and worried. They all knew that further abroad there were dark clouds gathering on the horizon. Greece's victory had embarrassed the Axis Powers, and Hitler had no intention of letting such an offence go unpunished. He had after all signed a Pact of Steel with Mussolini, which committed Germany to come to Italy's aid. Hitler's main focus was the Soviet Union, but Italy's loss made him turn his eye on Greece.

A German attack began to look imminent, and all Greeks knew that this would mean a war that they had no hope of winning. Amidst this national foreboding, on 29th January 1941, Ioannis Metaxas, fell mortally ill and passed away. Just over two weeks later, Turkey and Bulgaria signed a non-aggression pact with Germany, and two weeks after that, the news came that German troops were moving through Bulgaria towards the Greek border.

The Italians sensed the change of fortune and launched a massive spring offensive. It began with over 100 000 rounds landing on and around the Greek positions over two hellish hours. Villages was destroyed, trees exploded, craters were blown into the mountains. The Greeks lay on the floor and the earth shook beneath them. The air was thick with smoke. The Italians advanced, and as the smoke cleared, they saw the Greek army on its feet, ready, bayonets fixed. No advance was made.

The bigger battle however, now lay on another frontier. By the first week of April there were 680 000 Germans troops in Bulgaria and it was clearly only a matter of time until they crossed over.

A famous, open letter was sent from Athens to Hitler that week urging Hitler to avoid an unnecessary conflict. The letter concluded, capturing the national mood, by saying that there had been a time when Greece had "taught the world how to live. If necessary, it would now teach it how to die."

Much of the Greek army was now moved from the Albanian front to the Bulgarian front for what was to become known as the "Battle for Greece". Again, sadly, we do not know if this is what happened to Kostas. He may have been assigned to join that defence, but he may have part of the army that stayed to hold off any Italian advance from Albania.

On 6th April, at 6am, the German Ambassador in Athens called upon the new Prime Minister, Alexander Koryzis. He listed Germany's grievances against Greece, and then informed the Prime Minister that the German Reich had ordered its forces to cross into Greece, to drive out any British or Allied Troops and crush any form of resistance it encountered.

Germany's 21 Divisions that crossed over that day faced nine Greek Divisions. The Allied forces were rushing up the country to provide assistance to the Greek army, but it was too late. The Greek Army put up a furious defence, to the shock and admiration of the Germans. Even Hitler admitted that "of all the adversaries we had to confront, it was the Greek soldier that fought with the most reckless courage and disregard for death." But it was a hopelessly one sided battle. The Luftwaffe dominated the skies and turned Piraeus into a furnace.

By 18th April, the Greek Prime Minister and most of the senior military leaders knew that Greece was beaten and that the Germans would soon be in Athens. Prime Minister Koryzis could see no way to win, and yet he could not bear to surrender. On that day he drove home, locked himself in the bathroom and shot himself.

The Allied Troops and remnants of the crumbling Greek army fought the Germans every step of the way. The Matheous in Atalanti would have heard the terrible fighting around Lamia. But for the British and Allied Troops, for the Greek Monarchy and government, and even for the Greek army, the big question now was about how and where to evacuate.

The whole country appeared to be on the move. The roads were teeming with displaced people, carrying belongings in trucks, on donkeys and carts. The dangerous seas were over flowing with ships to carry people to safety.

For the Allied troops, it was clear that they needed to avoid capture so they could pick up the fight elsewhere. For the monarchy and the government, there was a need to preserve an independent Greek leadership that would be able to organise opposition and one day return to run a liberated homeland. For the Navy it was clear that they needed to keep as many of the vessels as possible out of Germany's hands. The Greek air force was anyway now all but destroyed. The major dilemma was faced by the army. Should they stay or go?

Many were ordered to go. Some chose to go: so that they would not have to surrender their weapons, so they could fight on other fronts, so they could one day return and liberate their homeland when the odds were more in their favour.

Many chose to stay: because they wanted to be alongside the Greek people as they suffered, because they wanted to protect them in any way they could, because the thought of abandoning Greece to the enemy was abhorrent, and because they wanted to begin the resistance here, as soon as it was possible to do so.

Kostas stayed. It may have been for the reasons above. It may have been to protect his parents, his two younger sisters and his younger brother. It may have been, because on April 21st 1941, when Greece finally surrendered, Kostas was in love.

X: Trapped in a War Zone

"Just recently, when I graduated, I happened to meet your daughter, Peghi. I don't know how, but from that first moment, I loved her." Kostas pours his feelings out into this letter, in the midst of the Greek Italian War on the Albanian front. "It's not just that I love her. Since I have known her, I have watched her, and this has turned my love into adoration."

His letter to Peghi's father is composed in high Greek, respectful, but clearly written with an overflowing heart: "I thank God that I have met her, and with your consent, she will be my partner for life. I will always be grateful that you have given me such a diamond."

It appears Kostas met Peghi Ventouri at a wedding around the time of the outbreak of the Greek Italian war, through his sister, Heraklia. Whether Peghi and Heraklia were friends before, or whether Peghi was one of the thousands of people displaced from Piraeus because of the bombing and relocated to host families, is not clear. What is clear is the impression she made on Kostas.

Peghi's parents were both born on different islands that had only become part of Greece decades after Greece became an independent country. Her father, Spyros Ventouri, was born on Zakynthos, which at the time had been recently conceded to Greece from Great Britain. Her mother, Irini, was born on Kalymnos, an Ottoman island that had recently been occupied by the Italians after the Asia Minor war. Irini's father had been a local diver on Kalymnos, and in a death rare in those waters, was attacked and killed by a shark.

Spyros was a specialist in setting up factories to process olive oil. This work involved travel. Peghi herself was born in the south of Crete, in 1922, when the island had been part of Greece for less than 10 years. The stories of the Cretan revolts against the Ottomans were still very much alive in people's memories. The island was desperately poor, and the people both hospitable and violent in the extreme. In the villages, the peasants' lives were barely distinguishable from the lives of their ancestors of the last 2000 years. There was, however, one major change happening around the time of Peghi's birth: the Turks were being forcibly removed. This was the other side of the massive population exchange after the Asia Minor war. The Greeks were removed from Asia Minor, and the Turks were removed from Greece. The largest numbers of Turks were sent from Crete, where the two cultures had fought, murdered, befriended, respected and hated each other, and basically shared the island, for centuries. In the first years of Peghi's life, the coastlines of Crete were full of families weeping at ports, of land and property being vacated, and of a sense of sour victory.

It was possibly this tense atmosphere, or perhaps the lack of schooling opportunities for the children, that persuaded Spyros to move his family to Piraeus near Athens. Piraeus, however, was also no place to raise children in the late 1920s. In the same population exchange that forced the Turks from Crete, the Anatolian Greeks congregated in Piraeus with whatever belongings they had managed to salvage from the flames of Smyrna. The suburb became a vast, overcrowded refugee camp, full of shacks made of tin and board, surrounded by muddy alleys with terrible sanitation.

So from there Spyros took his family to the British Crown Colony of Cyprus, and they settled. In the 1930s, the countryside of Cyprus still belonged to the ancient world. Goods were transported by camel and donkey. The agriculture, pottery and needlework relied on tools unchanged since the time of the Romans. Monasteries and churches dominated the hill tops. The villages were alive with the noise and colour of Orthodox and Muslim weddings and festivals. The towns, however, were a different matter. These were fermenting with calls for unity with Greece, and the British were increasingly suppressive in enforcing loyalty to London over Athens. Particularly, with regards to schooling, and the curriculum was controlled to instil loyalty to the Empire.

Those tactics were unlikely to have made much of an impression on the convent schooling chosen for Peghi though. Politics was mostly absent, and the emphasis was all on piety and prayer.

It was perhaps the combination of a worldliness learned from the roughness of Piraeus with the timidity encouraged by the sisters of the convent, that gave Peghi her powerful charm. Her eyes were respectfully down, but when they came up for a moment, they flashed.

She had a disarming ability to be both playful and proper. Even much later in life she could draw people to her, and within moments make them feel trust, ease and affection. At 18, these qualities were surely enchanting.

In October 1940, Peghi was visiting friends or relatives in Piraeus when the war broke out. The bombs were falling daily. The explosions and the terror in the frail, overcrowded housing must have been intense. Food supplies in the city were already running low. There was no way that she could return safely to her parents in Cyprus across the besieged seas. She was trapped in a war zone.

Then she met Kostas in Athens: a handsome, young officer who, according to his friend, felt an overwhelming need to protect others. The chemistry sparked. In January 1941, he wrote to Peghi's father. "Please allow me to congratulate you for having such a daughter. I am asking you to let me share your pride in her. I am asking you to let me love your daughter forever. I am asking you to give your consent for Peghi to be my wife."

So as Kostas watched the ships embark with many of his friends from the Greek army, including his brother-in-law, Nikolas Makarezos, he knew that he had to stay. But he must have been in a dark, sombre mood as he sat with Peghi and his family on the morning of 27th April 1941, waiting for the Germans to arrive. The fighting was over, and everyone knew that the Germans would enter the city at any moment. Then the news came that the German 6th Armoured Division was approaching the capital from the north. People watched nervously behind shutters in their windows. At 10.45am, the mayors of Athens and Piraeus and the commander of the Greek army garrison in Athens handed over the city to the German commander, General von Stumme. The Greek radio, which had been playing the national anthem all morning, was suddenly silent. Athens was captured.

XI: Love and Hunger in Occupied Greece

It would have been hard to make it a happy wedding. The swastika was flying over the Acropolis. The Bulgarians were ravaging the land in the north that George had once helped capture for Greece in 1913. The Italians were marching through Athens like victors, despite their defeat on the Albanian front. Food was becoming ever scarcer. Yet, the couple were in love, and even in dark times, there is joy in that.

Kostas had been discharged together with all fellow officers. The Greek army no long existed in Greece. Yet in the wedding photograph, he defiantly put on his military overcoat. In solidarity, Peghi wore a military shirt.

Kostas's parents, sisters and brother would have been at the wedding. Peghi's parents could never have travelled from Cyprus to occupied Greece. It is unlikely Kostas's grandfather and his

Uncle Pantelis were allowed to travel even from Atalanti. So it would have been a quiet affair, probably with minimal ceremony.

There was one Uncle that Kostas would have loved to have seen at his wedding; and if he could have come, or if Kostas could have even learned what his Uncle Manolis was doing at this time, he would have been inspired.

Commander Manolis Matheou was in occupied Paris in 1940, married with three young children. When he learned that Greece had been attacked, he made the painful decision to leave his family and find a way back to his homeland. There was no way to leave France legally, so he cycled from Paris through France on a bicycle, avoiding Nazi check points. He rode through Spain on that same bicycle until he reached Gibraltar, from where the British Navy agreed to take him as far as Alexandria. From Alexandria he got to Greece just in time to lead mine clearing that unblocked the escape routes for the Greek Navy. He fought in the Battle for

Crete, and once that dramatic fight was over, he once again found himself in Alexandria. It was there he proposed a plan to keep the seas around Alexandria safe for Allied Ships, but to realise that plan, he needed mine-sweeping ships. He devised and led a mission to occupied Crete to steal five vessels that could be converted to mine sweepers. He successfully acquired the ships and he oversaw the conversion himself. He was still commanding the last ship conducting the minesweeping as Rommel reached Alexandria in August 1942.

With the fighting now mainly on land, Manolis resigned his Naval commission and applied to join the newly formed Sacred Battalion: the Greek wing of the Special Air Service that had just been established by Colonel David Stirling. He was sent to Palestine for training in undercover operations and returned to join the Sacred Battalion for months of fighting behind enemy lines. He was part of the small teams that drove through the desert in jeeps blowing up railway lines, aircraft, destroying communication lines and attacking enemy convoys. His commander described him as a very angry man: angry that he had been forced to leave his family vulnerable in France. After each successful attack, he would mutter: "that was for my children." Yet there was nobility to his fighting too. One time when his team had managed to shoot down a Luftwaffe fighter plane, and they knew that the Germans were approaching fast, Manolis still insisted on burying the pilot, "because today we have broken his mother's heart."

Back in Athens, Kostas could know little or nothing of this. Perhaps he knew that somewhere Manolis was fighting. He would have been proud, yet painfully reminded that his own hands were tied.

Kostas and Peghi got married just as Athens was entering one of the most difficult periods in its long history. The collaborationist government was naturally unpopular. It was also under extraordinary pressure. It was expected to pay for the cost of the occupation, but it found it impossible to collect taxes, as no one wanted to contribute to a government collaborating with the Germans and Italians, and there was anyway little industry and no merchant shipping left to tax. So the government did the one thing it could: it printed more money, and used that to pay the Germans and Italians. As a result, hyperinflation kicked in and the money became all but worthless.

Kostas was entitled to a salary as a discharged officer. This was how the occupying forces had intended to keep the army quiet and subdue discontent. Now that salary lost all value. The same would have happened to George's salary as a school headmaster.

The Italians and the Germans were paid in drachmas too and so they found themselves in the same situation as many Greeks. A German General stationed in Greece said that his monthly salary was enough for one lunch in a restaurant.

So they turned to plunder. Food stocks were seized, clothes shops were emptied, all raw materials from textile factories stolen and sent home. Minerals from mines were handed over to German and Italian companies.

The most deadly effect of all of this was on food supplies. So the government imposed rationing. From October 1941, in Athens and Piraeus, the daily bread ration was 116 grams. Not enough to survive. By February 1942, it was 84 grams. The estimated daily need for a man is 2500 calories. At the start of 1942, the rations provided 204 calories.

The effect was catastrophic. Athenians scavenged the countryside in search of plants, nuts, even grass – anything edible. Starving children roamed the streets in packs looking for food. People sold everything they could on the black market: often their most precious possessions in exchange for one or two meals. In the walk from Omonia Square to Syntagma in central Athens, people had to stop every few paces not to trip over someone who had collapsed, dying of hunger. Men, women and children stood for hours outside baker shops in the hope receiving small pieces of vile bread. The streets were full of beggars. No one collected the rubbish, and children scavenged through it. Young men and women turned old in a matter of weeks. Pictures from orphanages at the time show living skeletons, draped in loose skin. A few of the children had just about enough energy to scream. Most were too weak to move.

Many of the occupying soldiers were also half starved. They looted blatantly, breaking into apartments and stopping people in the street to take jewellery and watches. Children would scramble around German soldiers eating olives so they could suck the stones once the Germans spat them out.

The long, hot summer was followed by a particularly harsh winter, with temperatures regularly falling below freezing. Wood was expensive and hard to find so the houses were not heated, and as the months of malnutrition had weakened immune systems, people fell ill with influenza and tuberculosis. They collapsed and died in the streets. Parents who had given last bits of food to children died in bed, leaving small children to fend for themselves. Conscripts who had fought bravely against the Italians on the Albanian front and had been unable to return home after the fighting, crawled and begged around the streets of Athens. Each morning bodies were collected. Families would leave their relatives' bodies at the cemeteries at night, hoping to keep the ration cards. Tens of thousands died of cold and starvation during the winter of 1941/42 in Athens.

Each of the Matheous who survived that winter would recall for the rest of their lives the pain and paranoia of those months. The sight of dead children on the street; the sick, swollen starved bodies of neighbours; the awareness that you are all dying and could die; the madness and obsession with food that comes with true hunger.

But for Kostas and Peghi there was an additional reason to fear. In the terrible winter of 1941/1942, Peghi was pregnant. Kostas had to find a way to feed his wife and growing child.

The famine affected the whole country, but those who could grow their own food had a big advantage over those in the cities dependent on now worthless salaries. The urbanised Matheous who had moved to Athens were therefore worse off than those who had stayed in Atalanti, close to the land. That was where Kostas now needed to get to.

Normal systems of transport had broken down. Shortage of fuel meant that public transport had all but ceased. To travel anywhere anyway you required a permit from the occupying forces, which would not have been easy for a discharged officer like Kostas. Yet somehow, he managed it, and by the spring of 1942, Kostas and Peghi were in Lamia. In July, in a hospital in Lamia, Peghi gave birth to a healthy baby boy, George Matheou.

With his wife and son now secure from the worst effects of the famine, Kostas could start channelling the anger that must have been building up over the last year. The Italians and Germans had invaded, ravaged, oppressed and starved his country. His own family had hung onto life by a thread. It was time to start fighting back.

XII: Joining the Resistance

In 1942, in Atalanti, Kostas may have had a chance to say goodbye to the man he was named after: his grandfather, Constantine. Constantine passed away that year at the age of 86. He had been born into a world of scarcity and hunger. In villages that were dark, isolated and unchanging for generations; where communication with the outside world was rare, and from where Athens appeared to be a remote, exotic capital. He had lived to accumulate wealth, to live in a large house illuminated by electric lamps, to drive in cars, and most importantly of all, to see his children educated and urbanised. If such a goodbye did happen between the two Constantines, the elder would likely have been comforted by the birth of his great grandson. He would also have recognised, from the stories still fresh in his youth, his grandson's calling to go into the mountains to fight.

Legends of the klephts – the guerrilla fighters of the 1820s War of Independence – were as romanticised in Greece as those of the heroes of the classical age. They had lived Spartan lives in the hill tops and mountains, periodically sweeping down to harass the Ottoman occupiers, and with some foreign help, had eventually managed to free Greece all together. They also fought incessantly amongst themselves and were seen as little better than bandits in the villages they relied on for supplies.

The early andartes – the Greek guerrilla fighters of the 1940s - really did resemble the fighters of the 1820s. They didn't have any recognisable uniform. They wore Greek, Italian and German uniforms, farm clothes and uniforms from old wars and struggles. Their weapons were a mix of whatever they could steal or whatever they could get their hands on – some had machine guns, many just had old rifles, perhaps from previous wars or hunting. They carried knives in their belts. They left sentries around villages to look out for occupying troops, but tended to sleep out in the open, or in barns and shepherd huts. They even rediscovered old lairs and caves used by the klephts of the 1820s.

They came down from the mountains into the villages, recruited men for the cause and demanded food and supplies. They recalled the noble tradition of peasants supporting freedom fighters, and like during the Ottoman occupation, the poor villagers were forced to share the little they had, and then live with the very real threat of reprisals for aiding the resistance.

In other ways though, the resistance in the 1940s was a mirror of its time and represented the divides that were soon to split Greece into bloody civil war. So when Kostas made a decision about whom to fight with, it was a deliberate one.

With the Greek government in exile and the collaborationist government despised, there was a power vacuum in Greece and the communist party slowly filled it. It had a moderate base of support before the war but then became the focus of Metaxa's clamp down in the late 1930s. Now it was free from that restraint, in the war years it began to re-emerge with renewed confidence and ambition, and formed an armed wing named ELAS, which proved more effective at mobilising and recruiting than any other of the disparate resistance groups. Crucially, it was also more willing to fight, which made it attractive to patriots who just wanted to get on with harassing the Italians and Germans, regardless of politics.

At its highest levels though, and permeating through the ranks, ELAS did have another agenda beyond fighting the invaders. It was a long term agenda: to ensure that the Greek government in exile, still populated by communist hating Metaxas followers, did not run the country post-liberation. Therefore ELAS had one eye on the Germans, and the other on any national rivals that might disrupt plans for a communist, post-war Greece.

The politics of ELAS is probably what deterred Kostas from joining it, even though it was the dominant resistance group in the region. He could have tried the other main group, EDES, which was saying all the right things to the British, who by late 1942, were parachuting people into Greece to arm the fight against the Axis Powers. But EDES's base in the region was weaker, and most importantly, it was much less inclined to take the fight to the enemy.

So Kostas chose a third, smaller option – EKKA, led by Colonel Psaros, who the British described as the most straight-forward, honest and honourable officer in the whole resistance. Psaros had one agenda only: to fight and remove the Axis Powers from Greece. In this, he was a man after Kostas's own heart.

At some point in the latter half of 1942, Kostas said goodbye to his wife and baby son and joined Colonel Psaros's resistance group based around Mount Giona. His life as an andarte had begun.

While it was still warm enough they lived in shepherds' huts high up the mountain. In the winter, when the snow fell and the wind bit, they moved further down, huddling in caves or huts, always staying clear of towns or villages that might be subject to random checks.

It was dangerous to be an andarte. It was also dangerous to support them. By late 1942, the Italians were scaling up the number of arrests of andarte sympathisers. Two hundred were arrested in Lamia. The Italians particularly targeted Greek officers who they thought may be tempted to join the resistance. Hundreds were transported out of Greece. Many didn't return. Kostas had got out just in time.

When the andartes struck, the response was brutal. After one andarte ambush that autumn, the Italians and Germans burned 29 out of 62 villages in revenge. It only fuelled the ranks of the resistance.

For the andartes, the skies were both a source of hope and danger. One day the Germans would drop anti-personnel bombs. The next a British Halifax would drop vital weapons and ammunition.

By late 1942, the British were actively trying to coordinate and arm the resistance in Greece. Most of the major acts of sabotage now involved British forces or at least British weapons. The most famous, the destruction of the giant Gorgopatomas Viaduct on 25th November, took place in Lamia, and it is very possible that Kostas was involved. The andartes attacked the Italian guards while the British laid the explosives. After a tense fire fight, the viaduct came crashing down into the river 100 feet below. The flow of raw materials to North Africa and Europe from Greece was reduced by 40% as a result. The Italians executed 16 Greek hostages at the remains of the viaduct a few days later.

Yet by the spring of 1943, Psaros and EKKA had to worry as much about ELAS as they did the Italians and Germans. Despite diplomatic efforts by the British to keep the resistance unified and focused, ELAS was becoming increasingly intolerant of other armed opposition groups, and on more than one occasion it tried to disarm

EKKA. ELAS was also growing, fast. EKKA on the other hand was becoming a small player. It was liked by the British, but was not seen as a force to be reckoned with.

As spring turned into summer, Kostas would have been relieved that for a moment the internal politics was put aside as all groups engaged in widespread action aimed at the Axis forces. The British supplied the materials, and the andartes carried out 44 major sabotages of rail and road and communication lines. It was a triumph of coordinated, disruptive action, and the andartes had much to be proud of. What they did not know at the time was that their action was a ruse, devised by the British to fool the Nazis into thinking that the Allies intended to land their forces in Greece and not Sicily. This was a tragic aspect of Greece's fate at this time. The various resistance groups were about to lock horns on the future of post-liberation Greece, whereas in reality, the fate of post-liberation Greece was never going to be decided in Greece or by Greeks.

Greece was a chess piece in the hands of the great powers

That though, is hindsight, and at the time, for those that lived there, the resistance was real, invigorating and the freedom of Greece depended on it. A British officer, Geoffrey Gorden Creed, recalls spending Easter in 1943 with Colonel Psaros and his men on Mount Giona. Kostas could well have been at the feast he describes. Huge barbecue fires were lit, young male lambs were slaughtered, the insides turned into sausages, their carcasses roasted, their hides kept for wine skins. They sat swigging ouzo and rough red wine. A variety of improvised instruments came out and the men leapt and swirled in wild dances. A swaying Colonel Psaros hoisted a Greek flag to a dead fir tree and the crowd cheered; eyes moist. From what we know about Kostas, he probably wasn't one of the men leaping around, but surely he was moved, confident in the cause, and perhaps impatient for the next action.

EKKA's days though, were numbered. In late July, Colonel Psaros and other EKKA officers, including perhaps Kostas, were high up on Mount Giona, encamped in shepherds' huts, training for the next round of raids and attacks. During the night, a large group of ELAS soldiers quietly encircled the camp and waited for first light. As the dawn broke, they opened fire above the huts and ordered the men out. Psaros could have put up a fight, but that would have meant killing fellow Greeks, and that was something he was not willing to do. So he conceded his stores and ammunition. It was a bitter blow.

Even more bitter was what was to follow. The men became restless. There was nothing for them to do without ammunition. Colonel Psaros felt that he had no choice. He disbanded his group, and told Kostas to go home and wait, promising him that he would be called again as soon as the British provided more supplies.

So Kostas began making his way back to Atalanti to his wife and son. He may well have been angry at Psaros. One British officer wrote that Psaros was courageous and good company, but that he was incapable of commanding 10 andartes, no matter a regiment. Perhaps Kostas felt the same way. Perhaps he was disillusioned with EKKA altogether and was already looking for another way to resist the occupation. He was about to find one.

XIII: The Hunt for the Andartes

Kostas would have had to keep a low profile in Atalanti, but at least he could spend time with Peghi and his one-year-old son. He could also catch up with old friends. Many of whom, by August 1943, had joined ELAS.

The Greek resistance had grown dramatically in the last 6 months and most of that growth was within ELAS. The majority of Greek men, and many women, trained or not, now wanted to contribute in some way to evicting the occupying forces. ELAS absorbed and channelled this energy.

Kostas's friends in ELAS had the desire to fight. They had the weapons and the energy – but they knew nothing of guerrilla warfare, and they lacked a leader. They urged him to join.

Kostas was explicit about his politics. He was not interested in fighting other factions of the resistance. He was not interested in laying the political foundations for a post-liberation Greece. He wanted to remove the occupying forces from his homeland: and that would be his only agenda.

It appears there was no objection. At the highest levels, ELAS was radically left wing and under the influence of people trained in Moscow. But at a local level, in 1943, while there was dislike for the government in exile and some excitement about socialist ideas – all of that was second place to the dignity of resistance. Even if there had been none of the ELAS propaganda and promises, the same people would have still wanted to fight the Germans and Italians.

So in August 1943, Kostas became the leader of the ELAS Guerrilla Forces of Goulemi of Lokris. In doing so he inherited a group that mirrored the community he had grown up in. Most were aged between 15 and 25. They were local farmers, agricultural workers, teachers and doctors. Kostas had just a few weeks to turn them into guerrilla fighters.

Time was of the essence because of the changing tide of the war. For the people of Greece, the occupation was about to enter its most violent phase.

After Greece surrendered in 1941, the country was carved up between the two occupying forces – the Germans and the Italians. The Germans were only interested in particular parts of the country and were content to leave the rest to be policed by the Italians. In mid-1943, there were 93 000 Italian troops in mainland Greece. Amongst them were some rough and violent men, but generally, the Italians were not inclined towards brutal punishments and not particularly oppressive. By August 1943, they knew anyway that the war was going against them and that Italy was on the verge of surrendering to the Allied Forces. Their commitment to the occupation in Greece was waning.

The Germans knew this too, and in the first half of 1943, the Wehrmacht Supreme Command ordered a build-up of forces in Greece: including a new Luftwaffe division, 117 Jaeger Division, 104 Jaeger Division, 1st Panzer Division, a Tank Division and the 1st Mountain Division. They would enforce a very different type of occupation.

Their priority was to crush the andartes. They instructed their men to stiffen their resolve and to rid themselves of any romantic delusions about the Greek resistance. Their orders were that all armed men were to be shot on the spot. Villages from which shots are fired were to be destroyed and all men taken out and shot. For any German killed, at least 10 Greeks must be hanged. In places, the order was increased to execute 50 to 100 Greeks for every German killed. The troops were "authorised and ordered to take any measure without restriction, even against women and children, if they are necessary for success." The Divisions themselves were populated by soldiers fresh from the most brutal fighting on the Eastern Front. Over the course of the next year they burned down over 1000 villages, looted and destroyed a million houses, and killed or wounded over 20 000 Greek civilians.

This was the force moving down through Greece in the late summer of 1943, reaping destruction as it went. This was what Kostas was preparing his men to face.

On 24th August 1943, Kostas scribbled a private letter and handed it for safekeeping to his Uncle Pantelis. He then left to the mountains for the second time. Only this time, he was in charge.

Perhaps the greatest stress for the andartes came from fear for their families. The threats to women and children were from all sides. Not just in the struggle for food and medical care, but from physical violence, either from the occupying forces or from rival resistance groups. By late 1943, the wives of ELAS fighters were becoming the target of the Security Battalion: a violent, Greek, anti-communist group that had at least the tacit support of the Germans. Many andarte fighters, particularly the leaders, therefore tried to keep their families close enough to protect.

Probably for this reason, Kostas moved Peghi and George nearby, into a shepherd's hut that he could keep an eye on and visit, and where others would not think to look.

During September of 1943, Kostas shone. He was tireless, enthusiastic and determined. He taught the men how to fight with knives and guns; how to camouflage themselves in the ancient olive groves; how to move along exposed mountain slopes in the dark and where to take cover and launch ambushes. The memories of him from that month are written with deep affection. He found ways to motivate, inspire and impose when necessary. Many members of his group would have still been teenagers, and Kostas was particularly careful to encourage and support these boys, who were probably away from home for the first time, and yet risking their lives. One of his men later wrote that you could feel just how injured Kostas was by the occupation and how deeply the need to resist was engrained within him. He "shared everything that he had learned from the people he had served with. He seemed to have drunk the spirit of his ancient ancestors."

Kostas pushed himself relentlessly, and by the end of September, "he had achieved the unachievable". His men were motivated and trained. He had designed a network of look-outs stationed around the area to monitor any movement of enemy troops and to ensure the safe movement of his own andartes. He was ready for the fight to come to Atalanti.

Kostas spent much of that month on the heights of Goulemi, overlooking rolling hills, miles of forest along the Atalanti plains, sunlight glittering on the Aegean and towering mountains in the distance. The intense heat of the summer was cooling into perfect, autumn warmth.

We cannot know what he was thinking. Perhaps, it was of the many times in history that his ancestors had come to fight from these mountains, against the Ottomans, the Venetians, against Pirates, Romans, Macedonians and

Persians. Perhaps he simply noticed how beautiful it was; and just when life was so fragile, he may have felt a fleeting happiness: that he was young, alive, standing before forests and mountains and being just the man he had always wanted to be.

Whenever he could, he would spend time with Peghi and George in the shepherd's hut. Their life there lacked any sort of material comfort. Yet many years later, when Peghi looked back at that time in the mountains, waiting for the few precious hours she could spend with her husband: she would say that those days – were the happiest of her life.

XIV: Fight or Flight

By early October, Kostas felt a heavy weight on his shoulders. The Italians had now surrendered and joined the Allies in declaring war on Germany. Most of the Italian weapons in Greece were quickly handed over to ELAS to avoid them being taken by the Germans. ELAS now had over 12 000 more small arms, plus machine guns and mortars. It was better armed than ever before. It seized this opportunity to issue orders to attack the rival Greek resistance group - EDES. EDES as a result began to open discussions with the Germans about their common enemy – ELAS. The German supported Greek Security Battalions were encouraged to intensify their attacks on ELAS and its families. The Greek civil war was already beginning. Communications moved slowly through Greece at this time and it is not clear how much Kostas knew of all these developments. Probably he was picking up bits and pieces of information. He perhaps sensed that it would soon become impossible to fight an honourable war in this resistance, and that this coming clash with the advancing German forces, may be the last chance to focus purely on the one enemy that mattered.

The news from the German advance was horrific. The German forces would encircle entire districts where they knew andartes were hiding. Once the area was cordoned off and all escape routes closed, they would send in tanks and troops into the villages: burning, hanging and executing. In the first week of October, they were just days away from Goulemi.

Then on 8th October, the call came in to the ELAS commanders. Starting from Lamia and encircling all the way down to Levadia and back up to the coastline, the Germans had moved 15 000 men and over 1500 armoured vehicles and tanks. They were advancing through the enclosed towns and villages: burning and executing.

That day the nearby town of Molos and its surrounding villages were put to flames. By the afternoon, the Germans had completed their encirclement of Lokris, including Goulemi. They were moving village by village, house by house, searching for the andartes and their weapons. Anyone harbouring weapons was executed immediately.

The villagers were frantically burying guns, munitions, uniforms and men's clothing in nearby forests. The ELAS troops moved higher up the mountains to plan the next move. Kostas's group was put in charge of the rear flank of the ELAS forces and asked to provide any possible protection to the villagers.

Yet once the various ELAS groups convened and assessed the situation, they concluded that resistance was impossible. They were surrounded, outnumbered and totally outgunned. They had nothing in their possession that could stand up to an armoured vehicle or a tank. They ordered their troops therefore to break up into groups of three or four and to hide out in the mountains and forests: to evade capture and to save themselves. They began to disperse in the afternoon.

All that is, apart from one group.

We will never know exactly why the 25-years-old Kostas refused the order to disperse and hide in the forests. It may have been his reading of the situation: that as the German encirclement was so tight and the chances of death or capture were so high; it made sense just to stay together and put up a fight.

It may have been his anger at seeing the German army ransack and murder its way through the villages around where he had grown up.

It may have been something more personal. Perhaps, he felt that he could never truly be himself again if he retreated now: that it would be a betrayal of the very qualities and values that defined him; and that it would be better to fall taking the right stance, than to live having taken the wrong one.

Or it may have come down to one, simple principle – that an invading army was crashing its way through Greece, approaching his home and family, and it was his job as an officer, a father, a husband and a Greek, to try to stop that army, whatever the cost.

Whatever his reasons, Kostas refused to hide with the others. He kept around a 100 men with him who were likewise willing to engage the Germans. K. Abrahams, who was one of those 100 men, later wrote that there was calm in Kostas that day, as if he had reconciled himself to sacrifice.

Our hearts, he wrote, were full of stories from the past; particularly the Spartans at Thermopylae, and of their defiance that was so powerful not because Leonidas and the 300 Spartans could inflict any serious damage on the giant Persian army; but because of the message it sent: that submission will not happen here.

Kostas's lookouts were still working, and in the early hours before dawn on 9th October, he led his 100 men safely high up to the chapel of St. Paraskevi. Each of the men walked into the dark, small chapel, permeated with the lingering scent of incense, its walls covered with the penetrating eyes of the saints, including St. Paraskevi herself, who time and again faced imminent death and was saved by miracles. They crossed themselves and prayed. As they stepped back outside Kostas spoke to each of them. He was calm, smiling, encouraging and joking. "We were all hanging onto his every word" wrote K. Abrahams, "and we believed that a miracle could happen to us too."

As dawn broke, and the mountains, the Aegean and the miles of forest were slowly flooded with morning sunlight, a lookout ran up to the chapel. He brought dark news. The German forces were encircling their position. Someone had betrayed them. The Germans knew exactly where they were.

Kostas must have looked back at his men and known that there was no way he could save them now. He ordered all the young boys, all the married men and fathers to scatter, immediately. He kept 20 men with him and moved down from the chapel deeper into the forest below, where they could conceal themselves and then find a way to distract the Germans.

The next few hours were hell. Mortars began landing from a nearby village. German aircraft began low sweeps over the forest. The earth was shaking from the sound of rolling tanks and explosions. Kostas couldn't know it, but at this moment, his lookouts were being captured and executed. Their positions had been betrayed to the Germans.

Thinking his lookouts were positioned as agreed, Kostas ordered his men to split up into two groups to make their movement less detectable. He still wanted to get into a position where it would be possible to engage the enemy.

With eight men, he moved slowly through the dense bushes: and straight into an ambush.

The machine gunner, John Loukavidis, automatically fell to this stomach and prepared to fire. He was killed instantly. Kostas whipped out his pistol and a German bullet smashed into the side of his face.

The German troops stepped out of the bushes. Their machine guns raised. Their fingers on the triggers. They barked at the guerrillas to lie face down on the grass. The men lay down. They had no choice. It had all happened so fast.

They lay, arms outstretched. John was already dead. Kostas was writhing in anger, clutching his head, his life draining out of him.

For a few moments the German soldiers lined up above the eight andartes; their guns pointing at the sprawled bodies on the floor.

Then, the German commander ordered his men to open fire.

XV

At that very moment, in Athens, Kostas's mother, Alexandra, heard her favourite, most beloved of sounds: those of Kostas's footsteps coming up the stairs; the distinct sound of his army boots clicking against the stone steps leading to their apartment. She rushed to the front door and opened it. The corridor was still and empty. She felt a deep, cold chill run through her. Slowly, as if in a trance, she walked back to the room where George was sitting. She placed her head on his shoulder, and weeping, she said "our son has just died."

XVI

There was a terrible, desperate knock on the door. Peghi looked up, startled. Germans? No, the voices were Greek. They knew her name. She opened the door and the andartes barged in. They were looking for anything that indicated Kostas was a solider: his sword, his uniform, medals, most of all, weapons: anything that could implicate Peghi as the wife of an andarte leader. The Germans were going house to house, arresting and killing. If Peghi was caught with these items, she would be taken out and executed immediately, or worse.

It was probably at this moment that Peghi learned that her husband had been killed; and now the andartes were fulfilling Kostas's final orders – to get his wife and son to safety.

Epilogue

There is a one more chapter in the story of Kostas Matheou and it occurs 45 years after his death. In 1998, Aliki Matheou, daughter of Kostas's younger brother, Alexander Matheou, was looking through a collection of books that had been in the Matheou household for decades. Inside one of the books, she found a letter, clearly scribbled in haste, dated from 24th August 1943. It was the final letter from Kostas Matheou, and it had never been seen since the day he wrote it.

The most likely reason for it having gone missing is that Kostas gave it to his only surviving relative in Atalanti, his Uncle Pantelis. After Kostas's death, Peghi and George were probably whisked out of Atalanti to Athens so urgently that Pantelis would have had no chance to give it to them directly; especially as the Germans were billeted in the Matheou family house. Then, in the thick of the civil war that occupied Greece for the next five years, it was dangerous to show even a family connection to ELAS. So, the letter stayed hidden.

In 1949, as the civil war was coming to an end, Pantelis witnessed the murder of a doctor in Atalanti who had left wing sympathies. Such violent events were sadly typical of the time, but the attackers nevertheless followed Pantelis and murdered him too, leaving his body in a nearby ditch. That way, the existence of the letter was forgotten altogether.

When she found the letter, Aliki contacted Kostas's son, George Matheou, now living in England. A few days later the letter arrived by post. George, for the first and only time in his adult life, could hear the voice of his father.

"My Dear Child,

When you grow up and understand how to read letters, my dearest child, you will learn that your father loved you very much, but just slightly less than our country.

I died for the freedom of our country; to get rid of a barbaric occupation, for the honour of our family and for you, so that you may grow up to be a great man.

My last wish is that you too become an officer and continue my work and our family tradition. You will then be able to understand why I gave my life and left you when you were just a little baby.

Dearest George, do love your mother who is now very alone in the world. She is a very good person and your father loved her very much.

When the time comes and you get married, don't abandon her. Let her love you and admire you.

I always loved you. When I was at home, I changed your nappies. I fed you. I took you out for walks and you were always sitting on my knee.

I must ask you my son, a Matheou, to grow up with honour and respect your mother. She will age alone and in old age she may become a rather nervous person. Be patient, because one day, you will also grow old.

I kiss you

Your Father,

Kostas.

Written on 24/8/41 on the day I left to join the Resistance in Goulemi

Annex 1

KOSTAS MATHEOU
(by K. D. Abraham, 1971)

Bold, you began, Lion of Lokris,
Seeking honour in slavery's darkness,
Hand held high like Leonidas,
To make sacrifice: a blaze.

You fell in Goulemi before you started,
Too quick to show you're lionhearted,
Now, let just ones, with wisdom imparted,
Cast you – with a look of iron.

My friend, I hold the love you taught me,
As mountains stand, so will your glory,
Children will one day read the story,
That you fired – into heaven.

Annex 2: The Story in Photographs

Constantine Matheou, (1856 – 1942) was the patriarch of the family that raised the first generation of urbanised Matheous. He built this house for his large family in the centre of Atalanti.

Constantine's eldest son, George Matheou, with his wife, Alexandra, 1912. George was mobilised to fight in three wars – the Balkans Wars, the First World War and the Asia Minor War. He was fortunate that he survived all three. Of the six sons of Constantine Matheou, only two lived to old age. George was one of them.

Alexandra's father, Panayiotis Kaloudis, was one of Greece's leading archaeologists. He gave his children a knowledge and love of history.

The Lion of Chaeronea was Panayiotis Kaloudis's most famous reconstruction. There is a museum dedicated to his work beside the Lion.

Anargiros Matheou fought in the First World War and the Asia Minor War. He died in his late 30s. Like many men of that generation, he perhaps never fully recovered from the horror he experienced in Anatolia.

Alexander Matheou had submitted his application for the third year of his law degree before going to Anatolia in 1921. He was captured in 1922 and never seen again. There is no information about how he died, but there were no good options for those captured on that terrible retreat.

Life goes on during the Asia Minor War in
Atalanti. George is headmaster of the local school.
The old school now houses the museum of
Atalanti. He is holding his young son – Kostas
Matheou.

Constantine's youngest children: Manolis, Evangelos and Pagonitsa Matheou. Manolis's heroic war record resulted in him being awarded the D.S.C. from Queen Elizabeth in England, the Golden Cross of Phoenix in Greece and the Legion d'Honneur in France. He retired from the Navy in 1947 as Vice Admiral. He died in 1998 at the age of 96.

Evangelos Matheou, however, died at the age of 26 in 1934. For a brief moment, he was a national hero when his plane crashed. The Aviation Ministry was only four years old in Greece and the few, trained pilots were in high demand. His death was a terrible shock to the Matheou family.

(From the left) Kostas, George, Nafsika, Alexandra, Heraklia and her new husband, Nikolas Makarezos. March 1940. By the end of the year, their worlds would be turned upside down.

Kostas Matheou. His course at the Hellenic Military Academy was condensed into two years so that he could be commissioned and sent to the Albanian front in October 1940.

Love in the time of occupation. Kostas and Peghi
Matheou's wedding in 1941.

The view from the Chapel of St. Paraskevi. Kostas would have spent the last weeks of his life overlooking these forests and mountains.

The spot where Kostas was killed on October 9th 1943. The dense trees and bushes made it a perfect spot for an ambush.

The monument to Kostas Matheou in Atalanti.

Kostas's son, George Matheou, with his uncle, Alexander, and his aunt, Heraklia, in Athens in 1946. The scene is peaceful but the civil war was already raging. Alexander would soon be called up to fight in it.

Initially, George, Kostas's only child, was on a temporary visit to England, but he ended up getting married and building his life in the UK. Here he is with his wife, Virginia, and three children: Constantine (named after his grandfather), Alexander and Helen (1979).

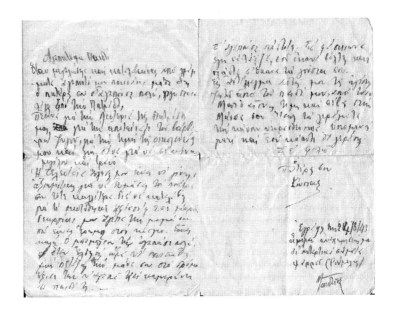

Kosta's final letter to his son was only found 45 years after he wrote it. It made a deep impression on the whole family.

Kostas and Peghi Matheou's great-grandchildren in 2010.

Sources

The first material consulted was a collection of family impressions written by my father, George Matheou, in 2002. These were inspired by a wider collection of Greek documents, articles, postcards and photographs about the Matheou family collected by George's uncle, and Kostas's younger brother, Alexander Matheou. It was Alexander's daughter, Aliki Matheou, who helped me understand and go through many of these documents. The information on Kostas Matheou himself comes almost exclusively from the articles of K. A. Abraham, who wrote so affectionately about his lost friend. I wish there was a way to thank him. His poem, "Kostas Matheou", translated from the original Greek, is included in annex 1. The historical background for this family story was collected through a lot of Google searching for old video footage and photographs; and from the books below.

Brewer, David, *Greece, The Decade of War.* I.B Tauris & Co. Ltd, London, 2016

Carr, John, *The Defence and Fall of Greece 1940-41.* Pen & Sword Military, UK, 2013

Clark, Bruce, *Twice a Stranger,* Granta Books, London, 2006

Clogg, Richard, *A Concise History of Modern Greece,* Cambridge University Press, UK, 2008

Creed-Gordon, Geoffery and Field, Roger, *Rogue Male,* Coronet, London, 2011

Gage, Nicholas, *Eleni,* Vintage Books, London, 2006

Hondros, John Louis, *Occupation and Resistance: The Greek Agony 1941 – 44,* Pella Publishing Company, New York, 1983

Kalyvas, Stathis, *Modern Greece,* Oxford University Press, UK, 2015

McMeekin, Sean, *The Ottoman Endgame.* Penguin Random House UK, 2015

Mansel, Phillip, *Levant.* John Murray, London, 2010

Mazower, Mark, *Inside Hitler's Greece.* Yale University Press, New Haven and London, 1993

Sarafis, Stefanos, *ELAS Greek Resistance Army.* Merlin Press, 1980

Toynbee, Arnold J, *The Western Question in Greece and Turkey,* Constable and Company Ltd, London, 1922

Sotiris Tsitipis, *O Eriokos Lokris,* Entoz, Athens

Woodhouse C M, *The Struggle for Greece.* Grenada Publishing Limited, UK, 1976

Woodhouse CM, *Modern Greece: A Short History,* Faber & Faber, London, 1998

Printed in Great Britain
by Amazon